OVERCOME THAT
SECRET ADDICTION

Overcome That

SECRET

ADDICTION

JEFFRICA WILLIAMS

Charleston, SC
www.PalmettoPublishing.com

Overcome That Secret Addiction

Copyright © 2023 by Jeffrica Williams

First Edition

Hardcover ISBN: 979-8-8229-1369-1
Paperback ISBN: 979-8-8229-1370-7
eBook: 979-8-8229-1882-5

DEDICATION

I dedicate this book to my grandma, Tecora Oliver, and Mrs. Cross. Both of these amazing women of God have gone to be with the Lord. They played a huge part in my life, helping me to grow as a woman of God. My grandmother would have cried to see me write this book. I had so much fun with this woman; she was naturally funny. I remember laughing my face off almost every day with her. Being in church with her was pure joy; she grooved to the choir like me. Grandma didn't mind telling the preacher, "Say that!" She is truly missed. Mrs. Cross encouraged me to use my gifts and talents to edify me for the glory of the Lord. This woman was incredibly sweet; she was the neighborhood grandmother. Mrs. Cross not only made sure I got to church and was baptized, but she picked up every kid that was willing to go. Praise God for mothers like these two women.

CONTENTS

Chapter 1
BODY IMAGE

Growing up, as a teen I was involved in different sports. It was obvious that I had a unique figure. Playing sports helped my muscles stay toned. I was a normal size, similar to other kids, so being concerned about my weight was not an issue at first. My body began to change around the age of fourteen. Not only from evolving into my womanhood, but also from unhealthy eating habits. This was the age I was when my dad reappeared back into my life. The previous summer I stayed over at Auntie Patsy's house, like I often did throughout my childhood.

This particular summer I returned home a bit chubbier. Auntie Patsy's house was so much fun; her daughter and I are around the same age. We found plenty of things to do, and auntie would make sure we ate a good meal. My auntie had a pantry in her kitchen full of canned goods, packaged goods, and junk food. For a kid, it was cool to see all the different snacks piled up on top of each other. If I asked for anything, she would grant me full access, but I knew not to be greedy. My auntie has always been sweet to me. Who wouldn't like to be around a nice woman with food? We didn't have a pantry in our apartment back at home.

My mom did the best she could with four children and no help from the fathers. Sometimes our kitchen cabinets would be full, and other times the cabinets would be short. My mom loved being in the kitchen. Cooking was like her therapy; I often caught her talking to herself while preparing dinner. She never used measuring cups or recipes; she cooked out of her heart. All the children call her Mama Shay. She had some greedy children; we were constantly running in and out of the refrigerator. She never restricted us from the kitchen. Have you ever been at someone's house and the kids are not allowed to open the refrigerator? Well, my mom wasn't like that. If it was in there, we had free rein to eat it.

Mama Shay has a kind heart; she was always opening her small home to other family members and friends in need. And, of course, they had to eat too. Whenever I close my eyes and reminisce about the soul food that came from her stove, my soul cries hallelujah. Mama Shay could have opened her own soul food restaurant if she wanted to. I'm from the South; we come from a family of great cooks.

The summer I returned home from my auntie's house, I realized my weight had changed. Others did too; my family is not shy to comment about your figure. People usually made comments about my bottom; I was blessed with a little extra back there. That's all of God's doing; he is very detailed in his creations. I can't do anything about it. And to be honest, I love my little extra. The same summer I returned home was the first time in my life I felt unhappy with my weight. My jeans had gotten so tight that anyone could have easily mistaken me as trying to be a fast young girl. Boys were not on my mind at this age; I just so happened to gain a few pounds.

Again, this was around the time my Dad came back into my life. Oh yeah, he disappeared when I was around eight years old. Let's just say it was a miscommunication of co-parenting, because I still don't understand up to this day. He was everything to me. My dad was very kind; he never yelled at me one time. He gave me some of the best memories of my childhood. It's a heartbreaking situation when somebody shows you things you have never seen before, then goes on with their own life as if you don't exist anymore. It doesn't make sense to me; I cried a lot for him. I often wondered whether he missed me or not. I frequently wondered if he was looking for me. There is one particular day that I still vividly remember. Apparently, I was upset about something that made me cry out loud, "Dad please come get me!" Temper tantrums arose within me as a child because I wanted him.

I longed for his scent; I wanted to see his mustache. Not only that, but I was starting to forget his face. Furthermore, I had no pictures of him; all I had to rely on was my memory. And to tell you the truth, my memory of him was slowly fading away. I knew he had to still be alive, and I remained hopeful to one day see him again. When I heard the news that he was coming to see me, I was super excited. Listening to his voice on the phone was unreal; he seemed so happy to hear from me. In all the suspense of this moment, I also remember feeling uneasy about my weight gain. This was the moment I'd been waiting for, and the enemy was robbing me of my joy. Great, my dad is coming, but now he's going to see what a chubby daughter I had become. I wanted to be flawless for my dad; at the same time I had questions. Thankfully, my attitude didn't ruin the moment of us reuniting.

My love for sports came from my dad's side of the family. Unknowingly, I played everything he did. As an athlete, it was not beneficial to be the big one on the team. There was very little playing time for you, at least in the sport of basketball. In comparison to the other girls on the team, I weighed a bit more than the girls my age. Most of the upper-class girls were taller and stronger. It's normal to compare yourself with your teammates; in a certain way you are competing against them too. These girls were fast and could jump high. Being fast wasn't my talent, but it was hard to keep up with me in distance. I was good at controlling my breath. As a matter of fact, that's how I won a lot of one-on-one competitions. As soon as my opponent showed signs of losing their wind, I would explode.

Because of my love for sports, dieting became a big part of my young life. At fourteen years old, I didn't understand how to diet correctly. At this age I became very conscious about my body. For the most part, I just didn't eat as much. There were times when I only ate once a day. Having strong arms was one thing that I desired. When they became strong and toned, I was glad about it. Exercising has always been a joy for me. Throughout my teenage years, my weight would fluctuate within a range of 130 to 150 pounds. My average weight was about 140 pounds. A chart that I once saw at the doctor's office considered that to be overweight for a girl of my height, which is five feet, four inches tall. I always thought God could have given me three more inches.

Because of my figure, a lot of boys in school had crushes on me. I want to say that's the only reason, but it had a lot to do with it. However, I was not boy crazy, I was more of a tomboy growing up. I would rather body slam him than have him touch my body. There was a time when I was walking to school at fifteen years old that two adult men were walking behind me. The conversation they were having was inappropriate and irrelevant, so I will not mention what was being said. It made me feel uncomfortable and disgusted. This is when I started to have the notion that all guys would only be interested in my body.

At fifteen years old, sex was not something that was on my mind. But it's the exact age I was when I lost my virginity. He was the Reverend's grandson at a church I used to attend. This guy was a few years older than me, a college student at a nearby campus in Memphis. I was surprised when he asked for my number. Prior to that we never held one conversation. Although he was cute and well dressed, I was not interested in him. I just didn't see him in that type of way. Who goes to church looking for love at fifteen? He made me feel older than my age. I was curious why he liked me. He must have had plenty of other opportunities, especially girls around his age. He told me he liked my eyes and my personality, but he didn't even know me. However, I fell for it; besides, he was a cute church boy, so he must be intelligent, right? At this age I had no clue about how to be in a relationship. I figured he would be a good boyfriend, and I had great potential for being a good girlfriend. I was a little nervous but excited to have my first boyfriend. The first telephone conversation we had was about sex.

Well, that day finally came; we told my mom that we were going to see a movie. Instead, we went to the Reverend's house, where he also lived. After a few minutes of that, I felt so stupid. Why didn't I say no? When a girl dreams about her first time, she imagines it to be romantic and pleasant. This moment was a total waste, and I can never get that moment back. Young women don't waste the most precious moment of your life. Even if the guy tells you that he really likes you. Wait on God! Let his compliments be just that, compliments. It does not validate who you are as a person. If you have already lost your virginity, don't waste your time on the next guy that pretends to like you.

From that day forward, I told myself I would never have sex with a man just because it's something he wants to do. This is my body, and I will protect it. I broke up with that guy immediately; he got not another second of my time. The movies people make sure do insinuate sex to look good. "I'm cool on this whole sex stuff," I thought to myself. After that experience, I could care less about a boy. Breaking up with a guy meant absolutely nothing to me. My friends drove me crazy crying over guys. I grew up without a father, so what's a boy? They couldn't break my heart; it was already broken.

Even when my dad resurfaced into my life, he continued to play the disappearing act. At some point I couldn't just blame him for the space in our relationship. We are alike in a lot of ways. One of those ways is if you don't call me, I won't call you. A woman once told me to take the lead and reach out to my dad. She encouraged me with her story. She told me she would walk around the neighborhood knocking on strangers' doors looking for her dad. That determined it for me; I knew exactly where my dad lived, and I had never knocked on his door. After hearing this, I took the initiative to reach out to him. I would call him and send texts and pictures, and sometimes he would respond back. Other times he wouldn't respond at all. And no, I was not getting on his nerves; these attempts would be months apart. I was not about to keep putting myself into predicaments that would cause me to be hurt repeatedly. When it's your biological father giving you no response, it hurts. Besides, I'm not wired to chase after any man. Forgiving people can feel like a hard process. Once I'm over the situation, I get into a protective mode. Whether it's the wrong thing to do or not, I'm still learning.

An important factor that healed me from that fatherless scar was finding out that I had a Father who would never leave me nor forsake me. That was enough for me. I will always cherish the moments my biological father gave me. My door will remain open to any moments he would like to create in the future. We are family, and I love my family dearly.

One thing is sure, I refused to let anyone's lack of responsibility cause me to be something other than what God has created me to be. Neither will they have the power to emotionally put me in a space that God does not desire me to be in. So that's why growing up I didn't care much about relationships. I could do without them; besides, I was just a teenager.

Chapter 2
HOW IT STARTED

I kept my body in shape by doing plenty of exercises and sports. When it came to diets, I tried them all: military diet, pescatarian diet, liquid diet, salad diet, vegan diet, keto diet, you name it. Praise God for growth, because today this girl does not do diets.

After high school, I received a scholarship for cross-country at a local college in Memphis. This was an exciting moment until I stepped on the scale at our first meeting. It read that I was 150 pounds. That number made me the heaviest girl on the team. Who was I going to outrun like this? I decided to get focused and drop a few pounds, so I would be able to keep up. At my first workout session I noticed a problem. I was extremely fatigued. Despite how I was feeling, I kept pushing. There's no way I was going to be the chubby one that couldn't keep up. "What's happening to me?" I thought. After the cardio warm-up, we went into a room to do exercises like a Zumba class.

All my energy left my body. When I got home, I tried to do a few sit-ups, but a sharp pain hit my stomach extremely hard. I knew something wasn't right. Unsure of what was happening to my body, I continued with some stretches. A few days later I noticed my breasts were sore. It must have been the Spirit of God that told me to take a pregnancy test. And sure enough, I was pregnant. I had no clue about pregnancy symptoms; I didn't even pay attention to a missed period. Oh boy, here we go!

Remember the part where I mentioned being cool on this whole sex stuff? Well, my senior year in high school, I met a young man. Hold it right here for a moment, let me take you back to the previous year.

When I was sixteen, I said a very small prayer to God. I always knew he existed, but I wanted to know more. For some reason, I felt like I couldn't receive more in the environment I was living in. No one in my house went to church, except me. As a child I used to walk to church alone; most times the church bus would come by to pick me up, from the same church where I met the first guy.

Going to church wasn't enough for me; I wanted to really know this God.

Sometimes Auntie Patsy would take me to church with her. Whenever I stayed at my grandma's house, she would take me too. And then there was Mrs. Cross, an angel God put in my life. She loved taking the neighborhood kids to church. She was our school's crossing guard. Mrs. Cross was probably in her seventies at the time; she was a very sweet lady. She took me to church all the time. I loved being at church, listening to the preacher, the choir, the Sunday school teacher, Bible study, all the above. No one ever had to make me go to church; I was up and ready on Sunday mornings. Meanwhile, people in my house were still asleep. Whenever I heard people talking about God, I was all ears. I wanted to hear the testimonies of what he did for them. Church was the only place I really heard about God, besides my grandmother. The first time I started to read the Bible, I was eleven years old. Of course, I didn't understand what I was reading, but I knew God was in it. If God is the creator of heaven and earth, then I wanted to read about him. If all the information I wanted to know was in this book called the Bible, then let me open it.

Yes, I did all of this, but I was still unsatisfied with not knowing much. Looking back in retrospect, God was calling me to have a relationship with him. There I was, sitting outside on the curb in front of my mom's house, staring into the blue skies as I often did. Even though I can't imagine what heaven looks like, I sure did try. As I looked up toward heaven, I prayed, "God if you meet me, I will come." Two weeks later my grandma came to pick me up to move in with her.

She lived in Jackson, Mississippi. My grandma was so happy to have me, and I was excited to be with her. Grandma was a member of a big church, and it was a lot of fun. They were always doing stuff with the youth. But I didn't want to be with the youth all the time; I wanted to be in the service where I could feel the movement of God. Don't get me wrong, youth church is good for a lot of kids. It was a little immature for me; I grew up with an old soul. I now see the distinctive roles God had my grandma and Mrs. Cross play in my life.

When I was going to church with Mrs. Cross, she made sure I was baptized. At my grandma's church, I somewhat knew what it meant to give my life to Jesus. Honestly, it wasn't until I sat down at her kitchen table with my uncle that I was enlightened about who Jesus really was. There was an unexpected connection God had waiting for me at my grandma's house. For the very first time in my life, at sixteen years old, someone finally broke it down to me. It was my Uncle Charles. He explained to me, "God sent his only begotten son into this world to save us from our sins. Jesus is the Son of God; he and the father are one." We cannot get into heaven without believing in the one who came to save our souls. I'm telling you bells were ringing all in my ears. My uncle surely had to be the answer to my prayer. God was meeting me through him.

My uncle is a minister; he and I have Bible study together until this very day. We don't rush it either; we are on the phone for hours on top of hours. There were days when we sat at grandma's kitchen table for five to six hours at a time, reading the word of God. Food nor water was on our minds; we were enjoying the bread of life. Uncle Charles really enjoys talking about the word of God. He never got frustrated with all my questions; in fact, they impressed him. With every question I had, he took me directly to what the Bible says. Presently that's how I teach people; I take them directly to what the word of God says. And the same questions I would ask him are the same questions people presently ask me.

The moment I realized that I had received the Holy Spirit was at the church he attended. I learned how to fast and pray; for the first time, I did three days and three nights.

Oh, a can of Vienna sausage never tasted so good in my life. That was the first snack I ate after the fast was over.

I learned so much in a short amount of time. Grandma wanted me to stay with her, but the school system in Jackson was trying to make me repeat a grade. As much as I wanted to stay, that was not about to happen. It really hurt my grandparents' feelings; they had made huge plans for me.

My granddad had a Burger King job lined up for me, and he was working toward getting me a car. Life was pleasant, I was attending a good church, plus my uncle was teaching me well. The atmosphere around me was calm. Nothing like what I was used to as far as smoking, drinking, cursing, fighting, and so forth. I was subject to stricter rules living at my grandparents' house than living at home, but I didn't care. Following rules was not difficult for me, especially if the rules made sense. Besides, I wasn't a child that needed much discipline. My mom raised me well.

I was always more comfortable staying home, even though my grandma wanted me to get out and make friends. She was concerned about me being bored, but it's hard for me to be bored. I guess it wasn't in God's plan for me to stay at my grandparents' house. I must admit, when I returned home, I was worried about my environment erasing everything I received in Jackson. One day I was in the shower praying in tongues, and my siblings made a joke of it, saying "she's been in Jackson too long." Well, I definitely did not return the way I left; I was now a saved girl, and I was not ashamed of it either.

Then here comes life, my flesh wants me to find out just how saved I am. First, it started with fighting; I couldn't understand the whole turn-the-other-cheek scripture. Girls at school had me messed up, so there I was, fighting again with my saved self. Now let's return to the part where we took a pause.

By my senior year I was ready to give the whole sex thing a try again. I'm telling you the truth, I would hear the voice of God whispering in my ear, telling me "No," as I participated in this sinful act. I felt horrible after the fact, but I continued to do so. There was a time when I cried while it was happening, but I still continued to do so.

This reminds me of Paul in the book of Romans 7:15, *"I do not understand what I do. For what I want to do I do not, but what I hate I do."* Do you see how temptation was waiting for me when I returned home? As mature as I thought I was, there needed to be room for spiritual growth. Instead, I immaturely fell into these traps.

Unsure about what he knew concerning fornication, I asked questions like, "You know we are not supposed to be doing this, right?" At one point I felt like I was putting him before God. I tried to end the relationship by telling him the temptation was too hard for me to fight. Unintentionally, I was breaking his young heart. He proposed to me after we graduated high school, but love was not in my heart like that. So now I find out that I'm pregnant. This shocked everyone, but not Jeffrica!

I asked my mom to tell my coach because I could not do it. They dropped the scholarship and told me I could try again the next year. For the second time, I felt disappointed in my poor decision making. The thought of becoming a mother overrode my feeling of disappointment. Rightfully so, I was super strict with my pregnancy. I read magazines and articles that explained what you should eat in order to have a healthy baby. First-time mothers are mostly concerned with bringing a healthy baby into the world. And I definitely wanted to do my part to nourish this developing fetus growing inside my womb. I ate plenty of vegetables, fruits, and that stuff they give mothers with little income on WIC. My sugar and junk food intake was limited, like a person with diabetes.

One day around my seventh month of pregnancy, I got a call from my dad. That made my entire day because it rarely happened. What he said to me on the phone changed my whole life. I was expressing my frustration to him about how I was gaining all this weight. "All I do is eat this nasty healthy stuff like these books say," I complained.

He told me in his country voice, "Jeffrica, you have an excuse to eat whatever you want. You are pregnant. If you want to eat a bucket of ice cream, you eat it. Don't worry about anything, you can lose weight after the baby is born, enjoy your opportunity to be greedy." Those words sounded like music to my ears. Believe me, I did just that; I ate whatever I wanted. During this pregnancy, my mom spoiled me rotten. She would cook dinner for the house and bring my plate to me. Sometimes when she came home from work, she brought me an Oreo fudge pudding dessert. My face lit up like a kid's on Christmas Day as she held that dessert out to me. Mama Shay bought my baby everything he needed: clothes, shoes, diapers, bottles, and more. She even threw a baby shower where the families of both the baby's parents were able to attend. We didn't have to buy that baby anything for the first four months of his life.

By the time I went to my final doctor's visit, I weighed about 205 pounds. The baby was not ready to come; he stayed in the womb almost another two weeks, and I gained about another ten pounds. Altogether, I gained sixty-five pounds while carrying him. My neck turned dark and rusty looking; it was easy to spot with my light skin complexion. I gave birth to a beautiful baby boy thirty-three days before my nineteenth birthday. My son was born via cesarean section. When it was time for me to take this baby home, I remember thinking, "Oh snap. You mean to tell me I got to take care of this little human?" Being a mom compelled me to grow up quickly. I told myself, "I'm getting a job and moving into my own house." I will create the environment I want my child to grow up in.

Before my eight weeks were up, I got a job at a Family Dollar store. I didn't tell them I just delivered a baby via c-section. They placed me right on the truck; I was lifting heavy boxes almost every day. At the beginning I was responsible for stocking the aisles. The incision on my stomach was being aggravated. Glory be to God, I remained safe. Instead of speaking up about my condition, I continued to work. I didn't want to complain about anything; I was happy just to have a job. They bragged about my work at the Family Dollar. The managers wanted to make me an assistant manager, but the district thought I was too young.

At this point, I was not concerned about my weight. I just wanted to provide for my son. Shortly after being blessed with a job, my son and I moved into an apartment complex. It wasn't long before his father moved in with us. He knew how I felt about shacking up, as the elders would say, so he proposed again. I'm sure he loved me the best he knew how, but I still declined the offer. Like I previously stated, love wasn't living with me like that. However, I continued the relationship for my son's sake. I wanted both parents to raise him, but that wasn't fair to me or the father. The moment I found an opportunity to end the relationship, I took it. I asked him to forgive me for being so mean, and I told God that I would never shack up again.

Working as a cashier at the dollar store, customers would ask me how far along I was. At this point I didn't even realize how big my stomach was. With a quick glance down at myself, sure enough, my belly was touching the counter. That cute little figure I had was gone. How could I even feel offended by the comments? It was true; I looked about six-months pregnant. So I decided to do something about my weight. "I'm going to get my body back," I said.

I was immediately determined to do whatever it took to lose the weight. Walmart had some dietary supplements that I thought would be good for me. The instructions said to take one three times a day, and I did. On the back of the packet was an exercise and diet plan. Step by step, I followed the plan. I also incorporated my own cardio exercises daily. Within five months I lost sixty pounds. All the weight I gained during my pregnancy was gone. My little four pack was back, and my strong arms were showing their definition again.

By this time, I had moved on from Family Dollar. One day I was doing an interview for a nursing assistant job and the lady said, "I want to swab your mouth for a drug test."

No problem, I opened my mouth as she swabbed the little stick around the inside of my jaw. At Family Dollar they asked me to urinate in a cup, so I was surprised by the whole swab situation. She said to me, "Let me do another one."

I replied, "Sure."

She then asked me, "Are you taking any supplements?"

I said, "Yes ma'am, I take dietary supplements."

She asked me if it was working.

I told her, "Yes ma'am I'm losing weight."

She told me that the drug test showed a faint line on the spot that indicated speed. I had no idea what speed was; but then I remembered from a television show I had seen that it was a pill that gets a person high. Shocked at the test, all I said was, "Really!"

It didn't keep me from getting the job. Either she believed my truth about the supplements, or they badly needed help. All I know is, I was working right away. By the way, I immediately stopped taking those diet pills. Drugs have never been my thing, and I didn't want the likes of it. Besides that situation, I also caught a urinary tract infection, but I blamed myself for not drinking enough water. Even though I continued to exercise, I stopped my diet plan. Soon, I noticed that I had gained a few pounds, which scared me, and there it started.

Chapter 3
IGNORED DANGER

Bulimia nervosa is an eating disorder followed by self-vomiting and extreme exercise. Those who suffer from this illness have an excessive concern with their body weight. They tend to eat large amounts of food, then shortly afterward feelings of shame and guilt take over. I know this personally because I suffered from this illness. Until this particular phase of my life, I had never obsessed over food, not even while being pregnant.

There's a huge difference between being greedy and being obsessed. I never thought in a million years that I would be sharing this terrible secret. This was something I kept only between God and myself. However, I said yes to God. I rebuke shame in the name of Jesus. I made a decision to allow God to turn my old secret into a testimony. So let me testify!

After losing sixty-five pounds, I was afraid of gaining all that weight back. I thought that whatever I ate was going to make me gain more weight. Eating healthy everyday was simply boring to me. Fatty foods were what I preferred. But my choice of food was not going to help me maintain my figure. Running on a treadmill was not doing me any good, as long as I continued to eat unhealthy food. The treadmill has always been my favorite exercise, but I became more obsessed with running during this period of my life. I could easily run six miles in one hour; as a matter of fact, I can still run like that today. Only now I do it for enjoyment; plus it's still my favorite type of cardio.

There's nothing wrong with wanting to stay healthy, but the minute we live in fear of gaining weight, that's a problem. One fact I didn't consider was that bulimia is a mental health condition. There was nothing about me that said mental illness. We usually think of a person with a developmental disability when hearing the term mental. That's not always the case; a highly intelligent individual can also have a mental health issue. How does this sound? There is nothing wrong with me, I just refuse to go to bed with this food in my stomach. That sounds crazy, right?

I'll even take it a step further; I didn't consider this to be a demonic influence. If anybody had told me that back then, I would have stopped immediately. I don't want to have anything to do with devils. But that's how the enemy operates, he wants us to think it's us making these decisions and not demonic activity. He also wants us to remain in silence; secrets get destroyed when they come into the light. As long as no one knows, they can continue to eat you up.

I knew God didn't like this stupidity. My actions were wrong, and I knew better than to behave in such a shameful way. I would pray to God, asking him to forgive me, before and after purging my food. You are always hungry when dealing with bulimia because you don't allow the food to digest in your stomach. Before I would even consume a meal, I knew that it was coming right back out. We can be so quick to judge someone else's sin, not realizing we do the same thing just in a different way. I recall a time when a lady was telling me that she would pray before she went out to sin. I thought to myself, "that's stupid." Well, how bright were my own actions just a few years before. Don't pass judgment, lend a helping hand. Prayer always works!

Besides the obvious sign of my weight dropping, my body began to react to this bulimic behavior in other ways, as well. Small red dots appeared in the white portion of my eyes. When self-purging (vomiting), you can put pressure on your eyes that causes the tiny blood vessels around the eyes to break. Of course, I was uneducated about this at the time. Bulimia can cause serious health conditions such as: ulcers, anemia, esophageal ruptures, stomach problems, damage to teeth, and heart failure. There are videos online that bring awareness to bulimia and inform viewers that people have actually lost their lives due to bulimia nervosa.

People don't usually talk about this type of addiction because it's quite embarrassing. This illness makes a person hide behind the walls of their home in shame. A teenager or adult can easily hide this addiction for years. Lord knows I sure did; I was fully aware that I was putting my body in danger. I ignored it, thinking I had full control of the situation. After purging for over a year, I started to feel sharp pains in my chest. I would stop, take deep breaths, and continue this stupidity. There was no way I was going to sleep with a full stomach.

Lord Jesus, talk about not realizing your blessings. Unhealthy, I lost about twenty-five more pounds. At this point I was even smaller than I was in high school. Once when I was at work, I went into the bathroom to purge my lunch. One of those sharp pains hit me so hard in my chest, I thought I was about to have a heart attack. I said a prayer to

God, "If this is it Lord, will you please let me into heaven anyway." I remember telling God, "This is the last time, I will stop."

If I had died from a heart attack that day, I'm sure the cops would have considered it suicide. Let me tell you something right now, the devil can make you commit suicide without having suicidal thoughts. Did you hear me? If someone overdoses from a drug habit, is that considered suicide? Well, it's the same situation. He is a sneaky devil; we must stay awake at all times. A next time is not always granted. That moment temporarily frightened me. Sadly, it was not the last time; and I praise God, he showed mercy on me, even though he knew it was not my last time.

Chapter 4

THE BATTLE

When I moved to Jackson, I became aware of how important it is to have a prayer life. So I prayed to God about my eating disorder, but not nearly the way I pray today. To help me fight against this addiction, I came up with strategies that only worked in the moment. Some days I ate less food, and some days I didn't eat at all. It's crazy how we struggle to fast as Christians for a great purpose, but the enemy can cause us to fast for an evil purpose, with no desire to eat at all. I continued to encourage myself while I was going through this storm.

In this testimony, I'm being completely transparent about my actions. Clearly I was having a war between my flesh and my spirit. I was extremely uncomfortable having a full stomach. You would think it's common sense to simply stop eating when you get full. But this illness is not formed to let you taste the addiction. The devil wants to steal, kill, and destroy. Here are some signs to look for if you suspect anyone you know and love might be suffering from this particular eating disorder:

- Going to the bathroom after every meal and running water.
- Using laxatives even though they have no problem naturally releasing their bowels.
- Using dietary supplements.
- Rapid weight loss.
- Not wanting to eat in public.
- Redness in the eyes
- Excessive exercising.

If you want to offer this person some support, you can start by kindly asking questions about how he or she feels about themselves. See how much that person is willing to open up. Don't push the issue if you see resistance; our prayers have the power to reach places we can't go. Mother, if it's your teenager, first pay attention, then get creative with finding ways of making him or her comfortable. It's called creating a safe space for them to talk. It's more likely to happen with girls than boys. There is a documentary on guys dealing with eating disorders as well. Men and women who are involved in sports, modeling, pageants, acting, singing, and social media, may suffer from it; it can have a negative impact on how a person views their body. It's a feeling of pressure to keep up. Eating disorders are secretive addictions; you will have to be around this person long enough to know there is a problem.

For over a year, I was single and living alone with my baby boy. Glory be to God, he did not allow bulimia to hit my life as a teenager. I probably would have ruined my chances of being a mother. About a year and a half into this addiction, I met a guy. During this time, I weighed about 128 pounds. I still had my curves; I was actually very pleased with my body at this point. As I was in the grocery store shopping with my auntie, I ran into this guy.

My goofing around made the guy smile. Now, I don't like to admit this, but I gave him a flirtatious greeting. In my defense I was just being nice. I didn't expect the man to ask for my number, but he did. However, I nicely turned him down. My aunt saw all this flirting going on, so she encouraged me to give him a try. She said one date wasn't going to hurt me. "He seems like a nice guy," she said. My auntie started giving him my resume: my niece is a good girl, she goes to work, she has her own place, she has one child, she goes to church.

I said, "Auntie really, I don't know this man."

He was appreciating all the 411 she was giving him.

My family was ready for me to find love, but I was okay with being by myself at that moment. People would tell me they couldn't believe I was a single woman.

In my eyes, I have always felt like a normal-looking girl, no matter who called me beautiful. My normal is beautiful, and I'm satisfied with that. The Lord gave me a good mixture of my parents. I have never been into fashion or jewelry that much. I'm cool with being comfortable, rather than girly. So when I met this guy in the store, he saw me at my comfort level. (That goofy, tomboy girl.) The red jogging suit I was wearing sort of hid my figure, so I knew he couldn't have been after my body. See how God works; he knows what I pay attention to.

After playing hard to get, I eventually gave him my number; besides, that smile he had on his face was adorable. For nine days straight we just talked on the phone; we didn't see each other at all. We talked for long stretches of time. The sun would be coming up on our conversations; he had a lot to say. The one thing that struck gold with me was that during our nine-day phone conversation, he didn't bring up sex one time.

"Oh, I like this guy," I thought. After two weeks I finally spoke up and asked, "When are you going to take me out on a date?" The first date we had, I put on my blue jeans, white t-shirt, and brown Timberland boots. He couldn't keep his eyes off me. When I caught him staring at my little extra, I thought, "Here we go."

Honestly, that was a turn off for me; maybe it hit a trigger from what I previously stated about the men walking behind me at fifteen years old. Although he didn't have a clue about that situation, he almost got dumped for it. In his defense he later told me that he was caught off guard, because he didn't see my full figure in that red jogging suit.

We built up chemistry over the phone, so I overlooked the direction of his eyes. It's funny when you find out this guy is a cook. It was his pleasure to serve me a plate. The first time he invited me to his house for dinner, he cooked lasagna, corn on the cob, and some type of bread. It was delicious; I kept that plate down.

We went on lots of dates; sometimes I purged the meal right in the bathroom of the restaurant. I would ask to be excused from the table and get rid of that food he just bought for me.

One day he asked to cook dinner for me at my place. I said, "Of course." He cooked me some jumbo shrimp, corn, and butter biscuits. I had never had a man cook for me. Well shoot, I never really had a man; I was only twenty-one. I started requesting his shrimp and biscuits because they were that good. Every time I ate that meal, I kept it down.

He wondered why I didn't have any food in my refrigerator. He didn't ask any questions at that time. He just thought maybe money was tight for me, as a single mom. Actually, I was doing well financially. Food was my enemy; I didn't want it in the house. Of course, the food wasn't the real problem, it was the addiction. The addiction was caused by the enemy. In my refrigerator was only enough food to feed my son; he was two years old. One book of food stamps would feed him for the whole month. When this guy opened my refrigerator to cook me a meal, there were fewer than ten items in there.

My mom would fuss at me about not cooking my son home-cooked meals. She was not aware of my illness, just as I was not aware of my lack of parenting. My son had everything a kid wanted and needed. Furthermore, I was a silly mom that loved wrestling and falling out on the floor. We had a ball, just he and I. One thing I didn't consider was my son needing to eat a home-cooked meal at night. He preferred the kinds of food kids favor, such as chicken nuggets, fries, cereal, noodles, sandwiches, and all that other stuff. Whenever my son went over to my mom's house, she would put delicious looking soul food in front of him. And he would barely touch it, so that's how she knew I was not cooking at home. Also, my auntie was his babysitter, and she cooked all the time. I figured he was eating well at her house and that was good enough for the both of us. Well, Mama no longer had to worry.

Glory be to God, this man he sent into my life made sure we had a home-cooked meal. I'm talking about real breakfast in the mornings: pancakes, bacon, eggs, and grits. The older people say, "The way to a man's heart is through his stomach." Well, that must be true for some women too, because he was slowly but surely getting to my heart.

As he was around more, he started to notice my frequent trips to the bathroom, especially after eating a meal. He never questioned me about it; I suppose he didn't want to rock the boat. Maybe it was uncomfortable for him, but I thought I hid it pretty well. But I was wrong; he knew about it. However, it didn't change his feelings for me. Despite having an eating disorder, I was still a great catch. He fell in love with me quickly; just seven months into our relationship we got married! I'll be honest and admit love still wasn't in my heart like that. I felt like I would never be able to fall in love, especially the way I heard other women talk about it. However, I wasn't about to let my cold heart stop this man from loving me.

He and my son had an instant connection. Moving forward, we bought our first house, and we were expecting a new baby that exact same year. The moment I found out I was pregnant, I tossed bulimia to the curb. If I wanted to put my own life in danger, that was my stupidity. But harming the life of an unborn child was not happening on my watch. Some stuff the devil just simply can't get a Christian to do. And for me this was one of those things. There was no urge to even attempt to purge. I had a goal to not gain as much weight as I did with the first baby. Throughout my entire pregnancy, I worked, swollen feet and all.

At nine months pregnant I out worked women who were physically normal. Even while pregnant I stayed in shape. I remembered my dad's advice, "Eat whatever you want." Indeed, I did! I wasn't too concerned about my weight; I enjoyed my pregnancy. This new husband of mine was cooking me whatever I wanted. Even when I didn't want to eat anything, he was still cooking food for me. I made a sarcastic remark to him, "You must want me fat so no one else could want me." He didn't seem to care how big I was getting. He told me every day that I was beautiful. Within a year of him knowing me, I went from 125 to 185 pounds.

During my second pregnancy I gained sixty pounds; at least I hit my goal by five pounds. Just two weeks after having my second c-section, I tried to start my exercises. The incision from my c-section started to hurt, so I begged off. Naturally, I lost all my baby weight in about three to four months.

The exact same problem started to happen again. Because of fear to potentially gain my weight back, bulimia resurfaced. Some days I would do well, and other days were not so good. I started to exercise past my normal workout routine. People were asking me for advice on how to lose weight. I told them the good things I used to do that helped me. This was not the time for me to give any advice. My body was looking good, but my soul was upside down. While I was struggling with bulimia, I was still living a decent Christian life.

Despite this issue, which I was dealing with, I was pretty strict about my lifestyle. (Talk about being double minded.) Usually, I didn't watch movies with profanity or sex scenes. I stopped reading sensual adult books at sixteen. My uncle told me not to read that type of book; he stated that they were not good for my spirit. I responded, "Yes sir," and never read those pleasurable books again. For a while I stopped reading books altogether. I didn't go out to clubs or listen to secular music. I barely even watched television. I've never done drugs or alcohol. Every blue moon I would have a cooler or a daiquiri. Drinking was never my thing; I have always been a coffee kind of girl. I started drinking coffee at nineteen years old while working overnight shifts at hospitals and nursing homes. I would read my Bible almost daily, and I only went to church or work, unless I went out to lunch or something with a coworker. To others this might seem somewhat like a boring lifestyle, but I was not bored at all. Feeling safe with Jesus is the most beautiful thing in the world. However, I was frustrated in the friends department; they became few to none.

Now I do not remember exactly what started this new, ridiculous adventure in my life. All I know is I did about seven months of backsliding. I turned away from my Christian lifestyle and even pursued a rapping career. The crazy part is I didn't even feel comfortable saying curse words in my own house. I would be in my house alone, writing songs, and whenever I got to a curse word, I whispered it. That's how I knew God was still with me. Subconsciously, I still needed to be respectful toward God, even if my actions were disrespectful. It's like when a kid doesn't curse in the house but as soon as he goes to school, he's cursing like a sailor.

The Bible says God will never leave you nor forsake you. My actions showed that I left him, but he remained faithful and forgiving toward me. It says in his word that he is married to the backslider. Jeremiah 3:14 states, *"Turn, O backsliding children, saith the Lord; for I am married unto you: and I will take you one of a city, and two of a family, and I will bring you to Zion,"* and Jeremiah 3:22 says, *"Return, ye backsliding children, and I will heal your backslidings. Behold, we come unto thee; for thou art the Lord our God."*

I tell you the truth; my heavenly father came back looking for me. When he arrived at my house, he held a belt in his hands, and I got a whooping!

Chapter 5
DELIVERANCE

Now, I'm not good with keeping up with dates, but somewhere between 2012 and 2013, I rededicated my life to the Lord. I was home by myself, which was very rare in my house. I was on my laptop watching rap-battle videos; I was getting ready to audition for one. Thank you, Jesus, that did not happen! A call came for me to audition about two weeks after I rededicated my life to Christ. Yes, he is an on-time God!

I heard that knock on my door. Hebrews 3:15 states, *"While it is said, Today if ye will hear his voice, harden not your hearts, as in the provocation."* There was a pull on my heart; that same day I listened to a testimony that made me feel convicted in my spirit. That was all I needed. I opened the door and allowed Jesus to come in and sup with me. I stretched out on my living room floor and cried like I never cried before.

My tears were uncontrollably heavy, with sweat and saliva running down my face. This was not a pretty sight. I'm so glad I was home alone because my cries were loud. It was like a kid getting a whooping from their mother. I kept repeating, "okay, okay, okay, okay." I cried these words of repentance, "I surrender God, I'll do right, I'm sorry, I'm sorry, please forgive me, please God, please."

I rolled around on that floor like I was practicing for a fire drill. I lay there sobbing for a couple of hours. You know that deep cry, where after you're done you can hardly breathe. Now, I'm not saying it took all of that, but this was personal between the Holy Father and I. Indeed, I went down a sinful woman, and I was raised up and created a new life. That old man died, and I experienced a purge that I never heard of before.

Can you stop right here and do a holy dance for me? Yes Lord! When I got off that floor, I was never to be the same again. That's what you call repentance. 2 Corinthians 5:17 says, *"Therefore if any man be in Christ, he is a new creature: old things passed away; behold, all things are become new."* God can make your addiction old. Let me say that again,

God can make your addiction old. Yes, that addiction, that secret addiction. When I rededicated my life to Christ, I rose up on fire. Honestly. I had to learn how to relax and maintain some earthly sense.

Everything looked evil to me; my vision was clearer than ever before. I threw away all my clothes, shoes, DVDs, CDs, makeup, jewelry, and whatever else I thought was unholy. I stopped reading my Bible and started studying my Bible. The Word of God continued to expose me. Whenever I thought things were good with me, I would come across something else that I needed to examine within me. See, I got rid of the external stuff, and God was showing me internal stuff. I went from dealing with a hidden addiction to dealing with hidden sins.

The deception from the devil was that I had no idea that these sins were hidden. Unforgiveness had tucked itself in the midst of my heart. The Holy Spirit guided me to all truth and spared no feelings. I needed to be righteous, so it was my responsibility to fix me. I couldn't blame my parents, my environment, my past, or anything else. I'm a grown woman now; I must account for my own life. So I chose to forgive and let go. Not only that, but there were lies that I had to uncover. Also, I had to lose the anger that was hidden within me. That was even harder than forgiving people because fighting was an easy problem solver for me. And, to be honest, it made my flesh feel better to punch whoever did me wrong in the face. I didn't realize my temper was still a part of me until someone activated a button. Furthermore, I had to get rid of my childhood behaviors. Talking about a clean house, I purchased a whole new one. God brought me out of Egypt!

See, when God brought the children of Israel out of Egypt, the whole point of the laws and commandments was to bring Egypt out of them. God had to humble them and test them to know their hearts. God is not finished calling his children out of Egypt. He is still humbling and testing the hearts of men today. Read the story about Moses and how God used him to deliver the children of Israel out of Egypt. Start reading the entire book of Exodus; take your time. Read at least two chapters a day. Allow me to share with you the revelation I got out of it.

Egypt represents sin and Pharaoh is the enemy, keeping the children of Israel enslaved to it. God is still pulling his children out of Egypt (sin) today. When the Spirit of God rests in you, he gives you power over sin. 1 John 4:4 reads, *"Ye are of God, little children, and have overcome them: because greater is he that is in you, than he that is in the world."* Mistakes will come and go, but as a new creature we no longer practice sin. Tests and trials don't stop just because we get saved. It's extremely important to have a strong prayer life.

The day I rose up off my living room floor, I was created new in Christ Jesus. Romans 6:6-7 states, *"Knowing this, that our old man is crucified with him, that the body of sin might be destroyed, that henceforth we should not serve sin. For he that is dead is freed from sin."*

There is a difference between committing a sin and serving sin. 1 John 2:1 says, *"My little children, these things write I unto you, that ye sin not. And if any man sin, we have an advocate with the Father, Jesus Christ the righteous:"* The beautiful thing about deliverance is that you do absolutely nothing. Jesus performs the miracle; he nailed our addictions to the cross. He nailed our bad habits to the cross. Everything I was doing wrong immediately came to a stop at the moment I got up. I was filled with the Holy Spirit, and a supernatural strength was awarded to me. Otherwise, I wouldn't have been able to continue in a lifestyle where I was worthy of being called a daughter of the Most High God. Bulimia was thrown into the sea of death, never to return.

That was over ten years ago. There was no more rapping, cursing, fighting, or any other bad habits I had picked up.

I continue to pursue righteousness daily. Of course, I have made mistakes along the way, but I intentionally practice the Word of God. I didn't need a psychologist or rehabilitation. I didn't need to be diagnosed or put on any medication. All I needed was Jesus! When you truly surrender, it's a new day in your life. He did it for me. I tell you the truth, an addiction is nothing but a stronghold. The reason why it's called a stronghold is because it's controlled by demonic activity. Demons are not weak, they are strong. They put their wicked power on the minds of God's children. They can't be talked to or medicated, they must be cast out. That's why we call on the name of Jesus.

Yes, Christians can suffer from strongholds as well. When I started to walk in my freedom, I forgot about this former addiction. I suppressed it until 2021, when I began to suffer from a battle in my mind. It felt like my thoughts were ongoing, and it was too difficult for me to stop them. I was experiencing pointless imaginations that meant absolutely nothing. I can't even describe it without it sounding crazy. I asked myself, "Who goes through stuff like this?" Daydreaming was happening all the time, even in traffic. God kept me from so many potential car wrecks. This was a secret I kept to myself, just like I did with my eating disorder. Finally, I built up enough courage to share it with my Aunt

Janet. She's my prayer partner. I needed her to touch and agree with me. Lord, I love how she is so understanding.

Everybody needs a prayer warrior on their side. I was looking to every sermon and motivational speech on the internet, radio, or in the pulpit to help me out. I came up with my own strategies, which temporarily worked. I tried to manage it, rebuke it, fight it; I even submitted to the confusion of it. This sounds familiar, right? I prayed over and over again. I quoted scriptures back-to-back. God was answering a lot of other prayers I previously prayed, but this one thing was still on me. I completely blamed myself for apparently opening a door that I didn't realize I had. Suddenly, I remembered that I suffered from bulimia earlier in my adult life. I thought to myself, "If God brought me through that, then surely he can bring me through this."

Again, I was reminded of those children of Israel when God brought them out of Egypt. They saw the powerful hand of the almighty God. They witnessed his miracles with their own eyes. As soon as they got to the wilderness, they built themselves another god. They forgot, that fast, how God delivered them out of Egypt. It wasn't until they were faced with another trial that they remembered Egypt. Think about it, they only brought up Egypt when they were either hungry, thirsty, or scared. When I was facing this new battle in my life, I sure did remember my Egypt. There were times that I was so mad that I prayed with my fist closed. With anger and tears dripping off my red face, I shouted, "Devil you got me messed up. I know how to fight." I would say a fierce prayer, and I believed in God for my healing. "It won't be like this always, it's okay," I told myself. Repeatedly I would tell myself, "You are okay." You're a king's kid, you belong to God, he sees you, and he will deliver you.

At moments I became a little winded from wrestling with this thing, so I decided to be still. I thought, well Lord, your word says, "stand still and see the salvation of the Lord." At this point, I can't do anything but stand. Then, in 2022, it all made sense. God had a purpose for my story. I'm talking about that secret addiction, which I had forgotten about. Now, why I had to go through this particular battle, I'm not sure. Maybe God allowed it so I'll have enough courage to be brave.

I made a statement to God, and I quote, "Lord, I'm not sure who I am going through this for, but I will tell it from the mountaintop, whenever you deliver me."

The moment I started writing this book, God freed me.

Stop for one second and do a holy dance for me!

We just went through my whole testimony, for me to witness to you on how God can take your secret addiction and turn it into a testimony. You don't have to write a book like I did, but you will help so many other people around you.

Are you ready for your deliverance? Right now!

One thing is certain; a person has to be ready to be set free. If you are dealing with an addiction, this is not the way God made you. That's a lie from the pits of hell. Life does not have to be this way for you. It does not matter whether your addiction is: drugs (pills), alcohol, gambling, gluttony, stealing, sex, pornography, television, eating disorder, cursing, or even if you are just struggling in your mind. Deliverance is here for you!

My Bishop always says, "God has a delivery date with your name on it." Now that you have made up your mind that you want to be free, your life will change.

Take these steps toward your freedom.

1. Discover the root of the problem.
    Where did this come from? Then deal with that pain immediately, release it. With this first step, you are already halfway there.

2. Acknowledge and admit (not that you are his addiction, but this addiction exists in you).

   By doing this we are canceling out the lies and deceptions of the enemy. No more, no more denials!

3. Read what the Bible declares to be true.

   Here is the problem in our world: a lot of people don't trust in the holy written Word of God. So, if that's you, then I'm sorry, but you must find Jesus before you do these steps. He is the one who sets you free. You can do that now by saying, "Lord, I believe in Jesus as my Lord and Savior. I believe that he died and rose again. Come into my heart and save me now. Forgive me for my sins and wash me clean. I confess with my mouth that I am born again, Amen."

   All right, now that we are all believers in Christ Jesus, let's start with the scriptures below. By the way, we have access to all types of technology to help readers understand the Bible. So please don't use the excuse that you can't understand it. Get some paper or index cards and start writing. Feel free to come back to this after your next step; whatever you do, don't leave out a step. Some scriptures I like to meditate on are placed in the back of your book.

- Romans 6 (read entire chapter, get your highlighter)
- Romans 8:5-9
- Romans 12:1-2, 21 & Romans 13:9-14
- 1 Corinthians 6 (read entire chapter)
- 2 Corinthians 4:3-9
- Ephesians 6:10-18

These scriptures will expose you to truth and give you courage to fight. Download these words into your spirit by continuing to study daily. This is your new prescription! Make it exciting; have breakfast with the Word of God. Grab a notebook and pen so you can take notes.

4. Are you ready?

Now open your door! (The door to your heart.)

Get in a quiet place: closet, bathroom, bedroom, or wherever it's just you and Jesus. Lie stretched out on the floor with your head toward heaven and weep for your sins. Don't hold anything back, let it all out.

Cry for your soul, confess your wrongdoings, apologize to God, and *repent*. If you need to holler, scream, kick, and yell heaven down, do it now. It's not crazy, addictions are crazy. This kind of prayer is called fervent. This is godly purging. Give him your pain, frustrations, disappointments, failures, addictions, lies, fear, rejections, and allow him to throw them in the sea of death.

5. Now walk in your freedom! You are now a new creature in Christ Jesus!

    I am thanking God for your deliverance. If you did the work, then you have diligently looked for God. I am so proud of you, and heaven is rejoicing at your victory.

    Listen to your favorite preachers and motivational speakers. Get involved in a good Bible-teaching church. Enjoy your life as the daughter or son of the most-high God. Be happy, God loves your smile, and most of all he loves you! Hebrews 11:6 says, "But without faith it is impossible to please him: for he that cometh to God must believe that he is, and that he is a rewarder of them that diligently seek him."

    You have been rewarded *deliverance*. I praise God for your victory. God bless you all, Amen!

MY PRAYER

Dear Heavenly Father, I pray for every reader that laid their eyes upon the pages of this book. Thank you for bringing deliverance to every soul in the name of Jesus. I pray for good health and strength to be restored in the name of Jesus. I pray faith is increased in the name of Jesus. I pray backsliders return home in the name of Jesus. Let the prodigal sons and daughters return, oh Lord. I pray hidden secrets and habits be turned into testimonies. Bring your people out of Egypt. It's time for Pharaoh to let us go. Help us not forget what you have already done. Forgive us for polluting the land. Forgive us for not answering when you have called. We shall rise, oh Lord. We have placed our faith in Jesus. We are overcomers, and we have victory in Christ Jesus. We are the blessed of God, and great is our peace. We are covered by the blood of Jesus. We are blessed coming in and blessed going out. You shall increase us more and more, and our children. Our little ones will be leaders. They will be raised up under the admonition of the Lord. No weapon formed against us shall prosper. We will be strong and of good courage. We apply the full armor of God, and we thank you for protecting us. We thank you for loving us. We thank you for saving us. May our souls cry hallelujah. Amen.

SCRIPTURES & EXERCISES

Scriptures to Help Strengthen Your Walk and Lead You to Truth

Psalms 71:1-5

In thee, O Lord do I put my trust: let me never be put to confusion.

Deliver me in thy righteousness, and cause me to escape: incline thine ear unto me, and save me.

Be thou my strong habitation, whereunto I may continually resort: thou hast given commandment to save me; for thou art my rock and my fortress.

Deliver me, O my God, out of the hand of the wicked, out of the hand of the unrighteous and cruel man.

For thou art my hope, O Lord God: thou art my trust from my youth.

Psalms 86:11

Teach me thy way, O Lord; I will walk in thy truth: unite
my heart to fear thy name.

Romans 6:3-4

Know ye not, that so many of us as were baptized into Jesus
Christ were baptized into his death?

Therefore we are buried with him by baptism into death:
that like as Christ was raised up from the dead by the
glory of the Father, even so we also should walk in new-
ness of life.

Romans 8:5-9

For they that are after the flesh do mind the things of the
flesh; but they that are after the Spirit the things of the
Spirit.

For to be carnally minded is death; but to be spiritually
minded is life and peace.

Because the carnal mind is enmity against God: for it is not
subject to the law of God, neither indeed can be.

So then they that are in the flesh cannot please God.

But ye are not in the flesh, but in the Spirit, if so be that the
Spirit of God dwell in you. Now if any man have not
the Spirit of Christ, he is none of his.

Romans 12:1-2

I Beseech you therefore, brethren, by the mercies of God, that ye present your bodies a living sacrifice, holy, acceptable unto God, which is your reasonable service.

And be not conformed to this world: but be ye transformed by the renewing of your mind, that ye may prove what is that good, and acceptable, and perfect, will of God.

Romans 12:21

Be not overcome of evil, but overcome evil with good.

Romans 13:9-14

For this, Thou shalt not commit adultery, Thou shalt not kill, Thou shalt not steal, Thou shalt not bear false witness, Thou shalt not covet; and if there be any other commandment, it is briefly comprehended in this saying, namely, Thou shalt love thy neighbour as thyself.

Love worketh no ill to his neighbour: therefore love is the fulfilling of the law.

And that, knowing the time, that now it is high time to awake out of sleep: for now is our salvation nearer than when we believed.

The night is far spent, the day is at hand: let us therefore cast off the works of darkness, and let us put on the armour of light.

Let us walk honestly, as in the day; not in rioting and drunkenness, not in chambering and wantonness, not in strife and envying.

But put ye on the Lord Jesus Christ, and make not provision for the flesh, to fulfil the lusts thereof.

1 Corinthians 6:19-20

What? know ye not that your body is the temple of the Holy Ghost which is in you, which ye have of God, and ye are not your own?

For ye are bought with a price: therefore glorify God in your body, and in your spirit, which are God's.

2 Corinthians 4:3-4

But if our gospel be hid, it is hid to them that are lost:

In whom the god of this world hath blinded the minds of them which believe not, lest the light of the glorious gospel of Christ, who is the image of God, should shine unto them.

2 Corinthians 4:7-9

But we have this treasure in earthen vessels, that the excellency of the power may be of God, and not of us.

We are troubled on every side, yet not distressed; we are perplexed, but not in despair;

Persecuted, but not forsaken; cast down, but not destroyed;

2 Corinthians 7:1

Having therefore these promises, dearly beloved, let us cleanse ourselves from all filthiness of the flesh and spirit, perfecting holiness in the fear of God.

2 Corinthians 10:3-5

For though we walk in the flesh, we do not war after the flesh:

(For the weapons of our warfare are not carnal, but mighty through God to the pulling down of strong holds;)

Casting down imaginations, and every high thing that exalteth itself against the knowledge of God, and bringing into captivity every thought to the obedience of Christ;

Ephesians 6:10-18

Finally, my brethren, be strong in the Lord, and in the power of his might.

Put on the whole armour of God, that ye may be able to stand against the wiles of the devil.

For we wrestle not against flesh and blood, but against principalities, against powers, against the rulers of the darkness of this world, against spiritual wickedness in high places

Wherefore take unto you the whole armour of God, that ye may be able to withstand in the evil day, and having done all, to stand.

Stand therefore, having your lions girt about with truth, and having on the breastplate of righteousness;

And your feet shod with the preparation of the gospel of peace;

Above all, taking the shield of faith, wherewith ye shall be able to quench all the fiery darts of the wicked.

And take the helmet of salvation, and the sword of the Spirit, which is the word of God:

Praying always with all prayer and supplication in the Spirit, and watching thereunto with all perseverance and supplication for all saints;

Write the scripture or scriptures that pierced your heart; use the space below.

____

____

____

____

____

____

____

____

What do these scriptures say to you?

What is your purpose in life?

61

Write how you spent your time in the last twenty-four hours.

____

____

____

____

____

____

____

____

____

After your next twenty-four hours, come back to this space
and examine your day.

____

____

____

____

____

____

____

____

List your goals here.

____

____

____

____

____

____

____

How do you plan to exercise your faith?

65

____

____

____

____

____

____

____

____

How has this book blessed you?

____

____

____

____

____

____

____

____

Write a letter to yourself.

____

____

____

____

____

____

____

____

Write a prayer to God.

ACKNOWLEDGMENTS

My life has been fully impacted by these wonderful men and women of God. Thank you, Auntie Janet, for your unwavering love and support. I admire your love for the Lord. You have been an angel in my life, guiding me, teaching me, listening to me, and even holding me accountable. You are my best friend; I love you, woman of God. Thank you, Auntie Patsy, for always making yourself available to me. You didn't have to drive across the city on Sundays to pick me up for church, but I deeply appreciate your sacrifice of time. I am forever grateful. You have no idea what it meant for me to see your vehicle outside every time you showed up.

Today you give my children the exact same joy you gave their mom. Tears come to my eyes as I think about your kindness. Praise God for aunties who show up. I love you, woman of God! Thank you, Mommy. Lord, this woman is so respectful and sweet to me. No matter what choices I've made in my life, you never judged me. You have always supported me through everything. You are the definition of a mother who never gives up on her children. The strong part of me comes from observing you. You taught me things in life without words. I love you, Mommy, stay strong.

To my amazing kids, I am one blessed woman to have little guys like y'all in my life. I thank God for allowing me to parent you three precious jewels. Because y'all have integrity and respect for others, it makes your father and I look like good parents. Thank you, my babies, I'm so proud of you guys. Thank you, Uncle Charles, for mentoring me and pouring the Word of God into my spirit. And, last but not least, is my loving husband. When I became impatient while trying to understand you, I asked God, "What is it about this man?" He replied, "He will love you unconditionally." And yes, you do! Thank you for being understanding through my ups and downs. You are one of a kind; I enjoy loving you and watching you be a father. I love how you adore me. Keep on cooking, baby; if your meals can win my heart, then America better watch out!

ABOUT THE AUTHOR

Jeffrica Williams is a wife and mother of three kids. She had a very normal and happy childhood, despite the difficulties she faced with her weight. Going to church was something she really enjoyed doing. Without being taught of God's existence, she already knew in her young heart that HE IS! She had a desire that lit a fire inside her to gain knowledge of this mysterious God. Little did she know, tests and trials throughout her life would give the knowledge to never doubt the power of the Almighty God. As she continues to grow, she is allowing God to work out her gifts and calling for his glory. She is determined to fulfill her purpose on Earth while encouraging others to do the same.

www.ingramcontent.com/pod-product-compliance
Lightning Source LLC
Chambersburg PA
CBHW061334120726
48001CB00002B/854